FINDING
Me

FINDING

Me

FINDING YOURSELF WHEN HALF *of* YOU *is* MISSING

Vickie Tingwald

XULON PRESS

Xulon Press
2301 Lucien Way #415
Maitland, FL 32751
407.339.4217
www.xulonpress.com

Paperback ISBN-13: 978-1-6628-1818-9
eBook ISBN-13: 978-1-6628-1819-6

Dedication

THIS BOOK IS dedicated to all widows who feel they have lost part of themselves and are searching for peace and a reprieve from an aching heart. I pray this book will bring you comfort and help you know you are not alone!

Finding Me was written for the wives who are doing their best to discover who they are without their spouse and best friend.

This book is dedicated in loving memory of my precious husband, Chaplain Gary Tingwald. I have been blessed with two great leaders and mentors in my life: Jesus Christ, and my husband, Gary. They both have led me by example, humility, and compassion, and have shown me an amazing amount of grace.

Table of Contents

Introduction

> *"Mourning is a constant reawakening*
> *that things are different."*
>
> Stephanie Ericson

G RIEF IS A strange beast we will all encounter at
some point in our lives. When loved ones leave us,
grief moves in and takes up residence in the heart. We will
grieve many losses in life, but none more profound than the
loss of a spouse. When you lose your spouse, your entire
world, and everything familiar, changes. Dealing with this
loss can be one of the most difficult experiences in your life.
While this book will be looking at the loss of a spouse, the
lessons learned about grief can apply to any loss.

> *"Grief is like the ocean; it comes on waves ebbing and*
> *flowing. Sometimes the water is calm, and sometimes it's*
> *so overwhelming all you can do is learn to swim."*
>
> Vicki Harrison

Grief floods in, unannounced, at unexpected times. It will sneak up on you and try to overtake you. It makes no difference whether the loss was sudden, or the result of an extended illness. You can never really be prepared. My husband fought a seven-year battle with ALS, a terminal illness, so we knew when death was imminent. We were given time to say all we wanted to say to one another and to say goodbye, but this did not diminish the grief.

Gary once asked me what I thought it was going to be like to be a widow. It was his way of preparing me. Looking back, I realize there was no way of knowing what my future would be like. There was no way I could have ever pictured "me" without "him." Only God knows all our days and what our future holds. I am thankful God is always preparing us for what He knows we will face in the future.

"It is hard to find 'me' when all the pieces are not there."
Author Unknown

Grief never attacks the same way twice, so you are never ready. This beast fights differently with each of us. I believe grief attacks in proportion to the depth of our relationship. It is not how long we have loved that person, but how deeply we have loved. My husband always said, "You can judge the size of the victory by the size of the battle!"

A widow's grief is not like other struggles you have faced in your life. It will feel like the loneliest road you have ever walked. Satan loves to make you feel isolated and alone in your struggles. Always remember, Jesus is with you and will fight the battle for you!

Our family and friends are there, but they often feel uncomfortable and awkward about our grief. Let them in, talk to them and help them understand how they can be there for you. If you feel you need to have some time to yourself, let them know that too.

> *"The darker the night, the brighter the stars,*
> *the deeper the grief, the closer to God."*
> *Dostoevsky*

Grief is a battle that is hard fought and never completely won. God helps by continually moving the battle lines back until there are fewer and fewer battles, and you find peace with your memories. Grief eventually becomes a familiar friend you can live with and accept. The feeling of your loss will always be with you, but God will give you peace and comfort. He will gradually restore your joy.

Grief will change you forever. It can make you bitter, or it can cause you to grow into a better version of "you." Grief is not a destination nor a place you want to stay, but a valley you must journey through as you move forward. Grief can make you stronger, wiser, and more compassionate toward others if you open your heart to God.

Your personal battle with grief cannot be, and should not be, compared to that of others. Every person will handle grief differently. God created us to be unique, so why would our grief be the same as someone else's? Eventually, the beast will lose its hold on you, and life will go on. You can emerge from the battle with a deeper understanding of who you are in Christ and who "you" are without your spouse.

Finding Me is a journey I am still on, but I can tell you each day gets a little easier. I have come through the battle and have fallen more in love with Jesus. He has given me a new hunger for His Word and a growing desire for a deeper relationship with Him. God has changed me and shown me how to view life from His eternal perspective. That has changed how I look at everything.

As you read this book, remember that many others have walked the same road you are on. You are not alone.

Grief – a new definition of self

I had my own notion of grief. I thought it was a sad time that follows the death of someone you love. And you had to push through it to get to the other side. But I am learning there is no other side. There is no pushing through but rather, there is absorption, adjustment, and acceptance. And grief is not something you complete, but rather, you endure. Grief is not a task to finish and move on, but an element of yourself – An alteration of your being. A new way of seeing. A new definition of self.

Author Unknown

CHAPTER 1

The Two Become One

❦

"And the two will become one flesh.
They are no longer two, but one flesh."

Mark 10:8 (NIV)

OUR COURTSHIP

G ARY AND I met while I was on spring break in my senior year of high school. Gary was from a smaller town, but was living in Des Moines, Iowa, where I lived, to attend an electronics trade school. He had graduated the year before. Ours was the classic "whirlwind romance." We met in March and were married in September!

The statistics for a lasting marriage were not on our side. We were both teenagers. I was 18 and Gary was 19. Our brief courtship did not give us time to really get to know each other well. Then, just six months into our marriage, Gary was drafted and sent to Vietnam to fight in a war. We were apart for the next two years. On top of that, my parents did not want us to get married. It was a miracle we made it past our first year with all those major issues. I would not advise any couple to marry having only known each other for six months, but it worked for us. We were happily married for fifty years and were only parted by death.

Our Marriage

Our wedding was simple, with few frills. Since my parents were opposed to our marriage, I had to pay for everything myself. Looking back, I realize what a trauma our whirlwind romance caused my parents. They wanted me to go to a computer programing school where I had already been accepted. But I was in love and there was no talking me out of it. My wedding dress and the bridesmaid dresses were rented. After the wedding, we had a small reception with cake and punch in the basement of a one-room country church. Then we were off on our "two-day-only" honeymoon — because Gary did not have vacation time and had to get back to work.

The Man I Married

We had so much to learn about each other! This man I had married was handsome, soft-spoken, and had a gentle, caring nature. I had never known anyone like him. Each day we were together, I loved him more. Our first six months were wonderful, and we were happy. Gary had a job at the Rural Electric Company, and I had a job at the bank. We did not make much money, but we had enough to live a good life.

Then, in the middle of our wedded bliss, a letter from Uncle Sam came in the mail saying, "Uncle Sam needs you!" We knew the letter was coming and had dreaded its arrival. In the matter of a few days, Gary was off to Fort Polk Army Base in Louisiana for his basic training. During the Vietnam war, you did not get a leave after basic training; you were sent to your next duty station. Gary was sent to Fort Sill Army Base in Oklahoma. He was told he would be stationed there and not be sent to Vietnam. I sold our mobile home, quit my job, and was off to be with Gary in Oklahoma. That only lasted a few months before he was sent to Vietnam to fight.

Gary was proud to serve his country, but we hated being apart. Before he left for Vietnam, we attended the funeral of his best friend, who had just been killed in the war. The funeral will be forever etched in my mind. What an awful thing to face the night before you leave for a war-torn country. His friend's mother was very gracious to us and felt bad for Gary and me. Gary had to leave the day after Christmas. The next chapter of our lives, and the letter writing, began.

"There are two moments in my life that I will never forget; the moment we met and the moment you took your last breath."

Author Unknown

LIFE'S BLESSINGS

Our life was filled with blessings. Yes, we had hard times, but the blessings form my most vivid and lasting memories. Gary returned safely from Vietnam, and we started all over again getting to know each other. Although we had been married four years, the war had separated us for two of those years.

Now we were ready to start a family. Our first baby was born on March 2, 1972. Deanna came into the world screaming and did not stop for over six months! That was difficult, but Gary and I both loved being parents. Deanna was a cute, chubby baby, and I was over the moon in love with her — crying and all! Then I became pregnant again. Because I loved baby Deanna so much, I remember thinking, *how can you have enough love in your heart for another child?*

On December 30, 1974, our next blessing arrived — another baby girl. Carrie was almost ten pounds! Her delivery was difficult, but that was soon forgotten. I discovered the love you develop as you carry your child in pregnancy is instantly magnified when the doctor puts that baby in your arms for the first time.

Our sweet family had grown from two to four very quickly. It was so much fun seeing how Deanna reacted to her new baby sister. She loved to hold Carrie and kiss her, and she was very protective. I think she thought Carrie was a doll for her to play with. I had to watch her closely, or she would just go pick up Carrie on her own. She was like a second Mom to Carrie. Once, when a neighbor came to visit, I noticed Deanna would not let the neighbor's little girl near Carrie. After they left, Deanna showed me bite marks on her arm. They were bleeding. I was shocked to find out the neighbor girl had bitten Deanna during the visit, and that was why she would not let her near her baby sister! I think Deanna still sees herself as her siblings' second Mom. That was alright. I needed all the help I could get.

Our home was filled with love, laughter, and life. Our next greatest joy arrived on July 28, 1977 — another baby girl! Melissa came into the world, and now my hands were full of three little ones under the age of five. Our life was hectic. We had moved to an acreage and had a dog, many cats, a pony, and were raising feeder pigs! What were we thinking? Shortly after we brought Melissa home from the hospital, I was going to get groceries. As we pulled out of the driveway, Deanna said, "Mom, aren't we going to take the baby?" I had forgotten baby Melissa in the nursery! Adding a third baby to the family, I discovered, was a big adjustment.

We loved living in the country, and the girls thrived there. Grandpa Tingwald thought Deanna, age five, needed a pony! What five-year old would not want a pony? She loved that pony and had lots of fun riding.

After about three years, however, the acreage had become too much to handle. We moved back into town just in time to welcome our fourth bundle of joy. After over 24 hours of labor and a c-section, baby David was born on April 5, 1980. This time we welcomed a 10-pound,

14-ounce baby boy. David was the biggest baby in the hospital nursery! He made all the other babies look so tiny.

When I was pregnant, everyone would ask if we wanted a boy this time. I seriously did not care if I had a boy or a girl. I had had some complications with two of my pregnancies and just wanted a healthy baby. With Deanna, I hemorrhaged and almost lost her in my seventh month. With Carrie, I suffered a stroke from the nausea medicine I was taking. A healthy baby was our only desire, and David was a healthy baby.

Baby David had an easy-going personality. Since he was our fourth, that was a real blessing! He was late in talking and when I had him checked, the doctor told me it was because his sisters did everything for him, and he did not need to talk.

Life was good and our home was full of children and love. I could go on and on listing our blessings, but I would have to say our four children will forever be at the top of that list!

"For you formed my inward parts; you knitted me together in my mother's womb. I praise you, for I am fearfully and wonderfully made. Wonderful are your works; my soul knows it very well. My frame was not hidden from you, when I was being made in secret, intricately woven in the depths of the earth. Your eyes saw my unformed substance; in your book were written, every one of them, the days that were formed for me, when yet there was none of them."

Psalm 139:13-16

CHAPTER 2

Be Good to Yourself

❧

*"The loneliest walk you will ever take
is the one down the road of grief."*

Author Unknown

MY NEW REALITY

W HEN THE FUNERAL was over and everyone
had gone home, I began to become conscious of my
New Reality. Up to this point, family and friends had occu-
pied my mind and my time. Many decisions needed to be
made. Going through all the motions of the visitation and
funeral kept me moving forward through the fog of overwhelming grief. But now, standing alone in my living room,
it all came rushing over me. How can I go on without Gary
in my life? He was the one I had lived for, loved, and shared
my life with. He was my best friend and love of my life. I
just stood there, frozen in place, listening to the deafening
silence that filled every room of our condo.

Our bedroom had been changed back from a room that looked like a hospital to what it was before. Now the king size bed Gary and I had shared was empty on one side. I could hardly go to bed for the pain caused by its emptiness. Our beautiful home, filled with life, love, and laughter just days ago, now loomed barren and still. How my arms ached to hold Gary once again. And my heart ached to tell him one more time how much I loved him.

Strange as it seems, my bedroom ended up being my comfort zone. Gary had seen Jesus there, and the angels had ushered him into heaven there. That gave me a peace I cannot even put into words. It was there that Gary took his last breath on earth and his first pain-free breath in heaven. All these wonderful and sad memories surrounded me in that room, and I felt the closest to both God and Gary there. The first year, I visited the cemetery at every major holiday and special event. But I never felt close to Gary there. I knew he was not there. Yet I could sense him in every corner of our home.

Those days following the funeral were the hardest. Coming home to a dark and empty house was difficult. When I woke up each morning, the reality of my loss would hit me fresh all over again. Everything I touched, everything I saw, and every thought I had were all painful reminders of my new, strange world. I discovered right away that I hated being by myself. I felt frightened being alone at night. After over two years, those feelings remain.

In those first days on my own, I kept busy with all the paperwork following a death. But all too soon that was behind me, so now what? I had to take care of all the

medical equipment we had, due to Gary's long-term illness with ALS. I sold our handicap van and donated all the
medical supplies. That took a couple of months, and here
I was again, looking at the walls and wondering what to
do with myself. Each new phase was difficult to deal with,
but soon passed to the next. Each month and year seemed
a little less painful, yet the loneliness and loss remained.
You learn to go on and make peace with your new reality.

God cares about what you are going through. Be encouraged, because through it all, God never leaves you. He sur-
rounds you with his precious love, carrying you when you
cannot take another step on your own. He is there, waiting
for you to share your deepest pain and sorrow. He desires
to be your everything. Lean in, trust, and let his loving
arms console you. Let him give you the peace and comfort
you so desperately need. He is truly a good, good Father
who loves you.

DO NOT RUSH GRIEF

If I could give one word of advice to a widow, it would
be this: *do not rush yourself* or allow others to rush your
grief. Often, people want to hurry you through your grief
because it makes them uneasy, or they just feel bad for
you. But do not rush the process. Take your time. Take
a step back and come away from the world for a time to
catch your breath and figure out where you go from here.
After all, every detail of your life has changed, or has been
affected, by the loss of your spouse. Since losing a spouse
turns your world upside down, it will take some time to

adjust. Immediately after your loss, you are in shock and just feel numb. It takes a while to realize all the changes that have occurred. Your social status changes. Your friends change. Your finances change. Your title changes from Mrs. to widow. The list goes on.

Each day, you are confronted with these changes, and grief can catch you off guard. This can happen the first time you must choose "widow" as your marital status on a form — before that reality has had time to sink in. Or when you are confronted with a problem your husband always took care of. For me, the first time I chose "widow" on a form was at my doctor's office. I started crying, and the nurse did not know what was wrong with me. I could not even speak to explain because of my emotions.

Then there are the car issues. Inspection, new tires, tire pressure changes for each new season. Who knew? You may need to learn how to do the simplest things — like pumping gas and doing all the driving yourself. Gary had always done the driving and gas pumping for me. I did not know some of these car issues even existed.

Who paid the bills? If it was your husband, that presents another set of issues to cope with. Gary was good to me and did all these things, but I was given some time to learn along the way, since he was sick for seven years. As he lost his abilities and was not able to do things, he would coach me, and I would learn. I had time and grew into some of my new roles gradually. But what happens when your spouse dies suddenly? You are thrown into a torrential storm of decisions and new tasks to learn. I cooked and Gary cleaned up the kitchen. That may seem insignificant, but believe me, it is not. When you are trying to cope with the day-to-day things, it is the little things that will set off waves of grief.

Some of the practical things you need to know when your spouse dies are passwords for the computer and cell phone accounts, banking information, how the bills are paid, and where all the important documents are kept (such as life insurance policies, title to the car, home financing documents or deeds.) Do you know what kind of final arrangements your spouse would want? What financial shape will you be in when your husband dies? Did your spouse have life insurance? Is there more than one policy? Where are the policies kept? Do you have a safe deposit box at the bank, and, if so, where is the key kept?

I have known friends and families who knew none of these things and had to start all over, setting up accounts and figuring this out on their own at the most stressful time they have ever experienced. A lack of knowledge about this information can cause more stress than you can imagine. Ladies, always allow your husband to be good to you and treat you like a queen but educate yourself on some of the important facts you will need to know if your spouse dies suddenly. If you have already been there and done that, then talk to other women who need to know.

Remember to take as much time as you need to grieve. When you feel overwhelmed, take a step back and leave it for another day. In the last year, I have learned most things can wait for another day. When we get exasperated and stressed, everything will seem to go wrong, and it all goes downhill from there. Remember: Do not rush your grief, learn to take that step back, and lean on and trust in God!

THE WIDOW'S BILL OF RIGHTS

I have the right to cry whenever and wherever.

I have the right to follow my own values and standards.

I have the right to my time.

I have the right to my own decisions.

I have the right to my emotions.

I have the right to my mind.

I have the right to ask for what I need.

I have the right to adventure and healing, especially when the two go together.

I have the right to make mistakes.

I have the right to feel afraid.

I have the right to feel angry at my position.

I have the right to be happy.

Author Unknown

Remember these rights as you go through the grieving process. There will always be well-meaning individuals who will try to tell you how to grieve. There is no right or wrong way to grieve — only your own way. There will be individuals who are uncomfortable with your grief and will attempt to rush you by saying you have grieved long enough. Again, grieve for as long as it takes and do not be rushed. Let God alone be your guide, shield, and defender as you find your way.

Just So You Know

"I cannot stop grieving just because you believe it is time for me to move on. I cannot stop hurting just because you do not understand the piercing pain in my heart. I cannot stop my tears from flowing just because they make you uncomfortable. My heart is not suddenly mended just because you believe that I have grieved enough. I will grieve the loss of my loved one for the rest of my life."

John Pete

"Just Be"

A few months after my husband died, I felt I should be doing something and not just sitting around. I had completed all the death certificate papers and insurance forms and felt caught up. Because Gary and I had always led a busy life of ministry, I was feeling guilty about not being productive each day. But, at the same time, I did not know what I could handle emotionally, and it left me feeling anxious. I was telling my oldest daughter, Deanna, how I felt, and Noah, her youngest son, overheard our conversation.

Noah said to me, "Grandma, you don't always have to be busy. Just take some time to relax and rest." When he spoke those words, they seemed prophetic.

The next day, during my devotions, I took the time to just sit quietly in God's presence. As I listened for him to speak to my spirit, I heard Him say, "Vickie, **Just Be** for a while." At first, I was not sure what that meant. Then I realized God was saying the same thing Noah had told me. It was alright to "**Just Be.**" **Just be** still and know He is God. **Just be** quiet in his presence and wait on him. **Just be** for a time and rest in the Lord. God was saying the same thing Noah had told me. I was to **just be,** and that was where God would meet with me and care for me. I had been so anxious; I had failed to stop and listen to God's still small voice. It took my precious grandson to remind me that it was alright to **just be** for a time.

"Be still and know that I am God."

Psalm 46:10

ACCEPTANCE

Often the first attempt to conquer your grief is to keep busy. You think the busyness will distract your aching heart. You soon find out that nothing can fill the void or comfort you. In those first few days after your loss, you are in shock and cannot think beyond your next breath. You are aware of what is going on around you, but nothing really registers. You are in a daze, with others making decisions for you. You feel good just to be able to dress yourself. Soon, everyone has gone home, and the hectic days of the funeral are behind you. This is the time the grieving hits you full force. You are left alone, struggling with the reality of your future. Now it is all you can do to just get through the day and the even longer nights. You realize you must face the rest of your life without the one you loved most in this world. Words cannot begin to describe these days. Your body, soul, and spirit are aching. You can feel a physical pain in your body you have never felt before. A pain caused by your grief. You try to be strong for those around you who are also grieving, but in the quiet times, when you are alone, you give in to your deep sorrow. Crying brings some relief, but it does not begin to quench the sorrow in your heart and soul.

These days will last for a differing amount of time for each person. There is no magic equation for the time it will take for your pain to diminish. Eventually, the waves of grief will subside and come less often. You will begin to experience life once again. You will come to terms with your grief in different ways and in differing lengths of time. You will begin to heal when you decide you must accept your loss, and your new position, and get on with life. The key to your healing is found in reading your Bible and asking God for strength, peace, healing, and restored joy. God will guide you, heal you, and give your life a new purpose and meaning.

> *"You will never know that Christ is all you need, until*
> *Christ is all you have."*
>
> **Corrie Ten Boom**

Along with acceptance comes relinquishment. Once you have found your peace in Christ through acceptance, you will need to take the next step and relinquish your life to God's design and plan. Catherine Marshall was married to Peter Marshall, who was Chaplain to the United States Senate. Peter died young, at the age of 51, and left Catherine a widow. In her book, *Adventure in Prayer*, Catherine shares her personal "Prayer of Relinquishment."

> Father,
> Once, it seems so long ago now, I had such big dreams, so much anticipation of the future. Now, no shimmering horizon beckons me. My days are lackluster. Where is your plan for my life, Father? You have told us that without vision we perish. So, Father in Heaven, knowing I can ask with confidence, what is your express will to give me? I ask you to deposit in my mind and heart the dream, the special vision, you have for my life. And along with the dream, will you give me whatever grace and patience and stamina it takes to see the dream through to fruition. I sense that this may involve adventures I have not bargained for. I want to trust you, God. I want to trust you enough to follow, even if you take me along new paths. So, Lord, if you must break down any prisons of mine before I can see the stars and catch the vision, then Lord, begin the process now.
> In joyous expectation, Amen.

When you have reached the place of acceptance in your grief, you can make this your prayer too. There is no better nor more exciting place to be than in the center of God's perfect plan and design for your life. This is where you will know perfect peace and sense the presence of God. You will once again feel alive and whole. You will be excited about each new day as you allow God to let his will for you unfold. Whether you are a young or an older widow, God still has a perfect plan laid out for each day of your life.

We can look at the life of the Apostle Paul for our example. He had a positive attitude on both life and death.

"For to me, to live is Christ, and to die is gain. But if I live on in the flesh, this will mean fruit from my labor; yet what I shall choose I cannot tell. For I am hard pressed between the two, having a desire to depart and be with Christ, which is far better."

Philippians 1:21-23

In this scripture, Paul is saying whether he lives or dies, he is content. If he lives, he desires to continue doing the will of God and to be fruitful for the Kingdom. Even in all his persecutions, Paul knew the number of his days were determined by God alone. So, as you continue living after your spouse dies, have the same attitude as Paul and desire to be fruitful for God's Kingdom. You still have time to reach many more lives with the Gospel in your days remaining on this earth, and your spouse would want that. You live with the same promise and hope of seeing your loved one in Heaven.

One day, you will stand before Christ and be held accountable for your life on earth. Not only do you want to hear the words "Well done," but you want to see many who have been touched by your life standing there in Heaven because you were faithful. It is my desire to have done all

Christ has asked of me and to have attained every reward possible. Scripture tells us we will lay our crowns at the feet of Jesus as our way of thanking him for all he has done for us. I want to continue making eternal investments with my life as my way of thanking Christ for all he has done for me. (Revelations 4:10-11)

GRIEF AFFECTS YOU PHYSICALLY

Grief affects every part of your life because of the stress it causes. You often forget to take care of yourself physically. Some of the physical symptoms of grief are increased blood pressure, body aches and pain, trouble sleeping, and waking up still feeling tired. Grief can compromise your immune system. Research done at Rice University in Texas claimed grief could even cause death. Grief increases body inflammation and that, in turn, can put strain on and affect your heart. Your response must be to take care of yourself physically during your time of grief.

If you have been caring for your spouse during an extended illness, you may have neglected taking care of yourself. This will look and be different for everyone, but some practical measures can be taken by all who grieve

1. **See your doctor** and have a physical check-up to make sure you are healthy.
2. **Get enough rest**. Lay down during the day if you are not sleeping well at night. Stress will cause physical exhaustion and we will need extra rest.
3. **Ask for help** if you feel you need it.

4. **People often bring food,** and you end up with way too much. Take it anyway and freeze it or ask a family member to freeze it for you.
5. **Take a walk** to get some fresh air and exercise. But most of all, just **be good to yourself!**

GRIEF AFFECTS YOU EMOTIONALLY

We all know and understand that grief will take its toll on you emotionally. Again, people will respond differently. Read the Book of Ruth in your Bible if you need some emotional strength to get through each day. (And believe me, you will!) This is the story of three women in the same family who became widows — Naomi and her daughters-in-law, Ruth and Orpah. All three women had lost their husbands, and Naomi had lost her sons as well. The story of Naomi and Ruth is a beautiful story of redemption. Look at this story and see how God faithfully cared for both Naomi and Ruth. It is interesting, but not unusual, that their responses to grief were not the same. Naomi's first response was to cry and became bitter and blame God. Ruth, however, responded to her grief by loving Naomi. She was determined, in her grief, to stay by the side of her mother-in-law, Naomi, and help her.

We can learn much from these women. Eventually, Naomi's heart responded to God's love and care. Their story began in tragedy and loss but ended in God rewarding Ruth for her loyalty and faithfulness, both to Naomi and her God. God chose Ruth, who was from the pagan country of Moab, and considered the "least of these" by the Israelites, to not only be part of the lineage of the next king of Israel, David, but also of that of our Messiah, King Jesus! Whether you are a widow or not, this story should be of great encouragement. God took two widows, an Israelite woman who became bitter and a Moabite woman who remained faithful, showed them love, and counted them worthy to be included in the redemption of the world. Always remember this story and be encouraged to know God works on the behalf of widows and will make every provision for your care.

Your emotional response to your grief is critical to your well-being. If you respond in bitterness, like Naomi, you will make it harder for God to heal you and may cause you to stay in your grief longer. Remember, grief should never be thought of as a destination, but as a rite of passage to a better place — place of great joy in the Lord.

"Praise be to the Lord, who this day has not left you without a guardian-redeemer."

Ruth 4:14

Grief Affects You Spiritually

When you lose your loved one, you often have many questions for God. Your heart is filled with "why." Death is never a welcomed event. It usually catches us off guard and unprepared. Even when you are expecting it during a long-term illness, you still are never prepared. You cannot "get ready" for death; you can only endure the loss when it happens. Many factors affect how we make the journey down the road of grief: our personality, previous losses, life experiences, coping ability, beliefs, and the relationship we have with Christ. Because so many factors play a part, we will all process grief differently

The story of Naomi and Ruth, the two widows in the Bible, shows how each responded differently to her grief and how it affected them. They were women of different ages, social, ethnic, and religious backgrounds. Naomi was suffering the loss of her husband and her two sons. Naomi had been forced to leave her home, family, and country to live in a foreign land because of a drought. Ruth had left her family and had adopted the faith and culture of her husband. Now that the men of the family were gone, they had no income or way to support themselves. Both women, like many of us who have suffered loss, had major issues they would need to deal with while walking down the road of grief. Grief can leave you reeling in doubt and fear. Ruth and Naomi each dealt with grief in her own way and time, but both sought God for direction and comfort.

At times of great loss, we need to depend on God more than ever. He alone can give the strength you need just to get out of bed some days. God tells us not to fear, but to be bold and courageous. Your confidence in times of great loss will depend on your relationship with your God, just as it did for Ruth and Naomi. The Word of God tells us not to be afraid.

"Peace I leave with you; my peace I give to you. Not as the world gives do I give to you. Let not your hearts be troubled, neither let them be afraid."

John 14:27

In Luke 21:1-6, we find the story of another widow in the Bible. We are not given the widow's name; we are only told about her giving. On this occasion, Jesus was sitting where he could see people putting their offerings in the temple treasury. He saw how the rich gave. He also noticed a certain poor widow placing two exceedingly small coins in the offering. Jesus responded by saying,

"Truly I tell you; this poor widow has put more in than all the others. All these people gave their gifts out of their wealth; but she out of her poverty put in all she had to live on."

Luke 21:3-4 (NIV).

John Wesley had this to say about the widow: "See what judgement is cast on the most precious, outward actions by the Judge of us all! And how acceptable to him is the smallest, which springs from self-denying love."

Jesus is making the point that our giving is not measured by how much we give, but by how much we have left over. In her pure love for God, the widow was willing to sacrifice all she had to live on. The rich gave out of their wealth and abundance, which cost them nothing as a sacrifice.

As widows, we can relate to this lady and her giving. You see, she trusted God with all she had. Do you trust God the same way? What are you willing to give God? It is not just about money. Are you willing to trust God with your future, your finances, your care, your love, and all that you are or ever want to become? God wants you to give Him your all. He wants you to have a generous spirit in all things. When you give God your all, you will never be disappointed. He will be there to meet every need you have. In your time of grief, he will be there to comfort you. He will never leave you nor forsake you.

Over the last few years, as I have seen God care for me and my family, I am amazed by his love and attention to every detail of our lives. His faithfulness has caused me to trust Him more, depend on Him more, and love Him with all that I am. God wants you to trust Him with your future.

God knows your needs as a widow, and He desires to be all that you need. He desires to come along side you with His care and abundance. He will give you the increase in every area of your life, if you will give like the widow who gave him her all. Trust God in everything, and your doubts and fears will be replaced by a greater faith in the one who loves you most!

"When we are powerless to do a thing, it is a great joy that we can come and step inside the ability of Jesus."
Corrie Ten Boom

STAGES OF GRIEF

Most people are aware of the stages of grief. Those stages are real and true, but different for each of us. The stages of grief are:

Shock and Denial
Pain and Guilt
Anger and Bargaining
Depression
Acceptance

Depending on where you get your information, the stages can vary in number. But these are the basic stages. Be aware that your grief experiences will not follow any given order. These stages can happen at different times, and you may go through them more than once.

My experience came in losing my husband after a seven-year battle with ALS. We experienced grief with every loss his disease caused. My husband first lost his ability to swallow and eat and had to go on a feeding tube. Then he lost his ability to speak. The next major hurdle came when he could no longer walk and had to start using a wheelchair. Next was when his lung capacity and breathing were affected. He had a trach put into his throat to be hooked up to a ventilator to help him breathe. The final loss was the use of his hands. For the last three months of his life, he could not communicate at all. ALS is a brutal and cruel disease. You stand helplessly by and watch your precious loved one lose every bodily function, until he is left fully cognitive but trapped in his own body.

My husband and I were grieving some loss all through his illness. I knew I had experienced the entire range of grief long before my husband passed. It did not make the grief any easier after he was gone, but I had worked my way through the shock, bargaining, and acceptance of his disease before he left us.

The strange thing about grief is, it does not care what the books say! Grief is that unfair beast I mentioned in the introduction to this book. It will attack you again and again from every stage. I experienced the stages of grief more than once. The easiest for me, after losing Gary, was the acceptance stage. God had dealt with Gary and me both about acceptance during his illness. God had helped us find peace and acceptance without having all the "whys" answered. By the time Gary lost his battle, God had given us both an understanding and acceptance in our spirits, as best you can have on this side of heaven. But the pain and loss were still just as brutal.

We will all have differing experiences with death, so the grief process will not be the same for everyone. You might not go through the steps in a certain order or even experience them all. Like my experience, you may go through some of the stages more than once. Grief is a hard-fought and lonely battle, but you will get through it and be stronger for your journey. Know that you will be alright as you move through the stages on the time schedule God has designed just for you. You will have victory through the strength of Christ who lives in you!

"May the God of hope fill you with all joy and peace in believing, so that by the power of the Holy Spirit you my abound in hope.

Romans 15:13

WHAT IS NORMAL GRIEF ?

Remember, grief is not a place to stay; it is a passage to another chapter of your life. Holding on to the past too tightly, or being stuck there, is a sign your grief is not moving in the right direction. If you resist your new identity and refuse to move on in your new normal, you may need to see a counselor for some help and guidance.

You may also need help if you are isolating yourself and pulling away from your friends and family. These are normal responses, but not if you are stuck in the same place and refuse to move forward. Isolation is a scheme of the enemy of our souls and will only serve to make your grief more difficult. We all need other people in our lives. Your family, friends, and church family all want to be there for you. Find someone you can talk to and trust, then see or talk to that person on a regular basis. Reading your Bible and spending time in prayer is also a path to healing.

Do not let your emotional pain cause you to lose touch with reality. It is normal to talk to your deceased spouse, but it is not normal to hold onto a relationship that is not real. Do not allow yourself to become a victim of your grief. Grief will take you captive if you let it. Take time each day to focus on the positive. The first year after my husband died, I wrote five things I was thankful for in my journal each day. Journaling each day is a great way to release your grief and anxiety.

Your grief is not progressing normally if you are having trouble adjusting to the changes in your daily routine. Life never goes on the same after you experience the loss of a loved one, especially a spouse you lived with every day. Your routine will need to be adjusted. I found my routine changed drastically because I had been my husband's caregiver. We had nurses, social workers, chaplains, ministers, friends, family, and hospice workers in and out of our house daily. The routine care for my husband was ongoing all day since he was not able to do anything for himself. He had to be moved out of bed each day using a Hoyer lift. He had to be taken to the bathroom, bathed, shaved, and dressed each day by me or an aide. Then his trach had to be cleaned before he was fed through a feeding tube and given his medicine. You get the picture. I went from a hectic daily routine of care, and a steady stream of people in and out of the house, to complete silence and no one there but me. That adjustment took some time and getting used to.

I had never lived on my own from the time I left my parent's home to get married until now. I lived with the same man for 50 years. Marriage itself was a huge adjustment. But I knew I had to make changes to move on. There was no other choice. If you are stuck in the same routine and cannot move on, you may need to talk to someone. Do not forget your pastor. He or she is there to support you. The pastor's office is a great place to start asking for help.

This takes me to the reason I am writing this book. I was caught off guard by the changes in "Me." Who was I without my husband? I began learning things about myself I had never realized. Two areas came into focus.

1. I never realized how much I depended on my husband in social settings. He was a minister, so we were in the scrutinizing public eye weekly. I depended on him for much of the social interaction.
2. I was not the "people" person I had always thought I was. Without my husband by my side, being around people for any length of time wore me out.

The most amazing discovery was finding how difficult it was to go to church by myself. The church had been the center of our lives, calling, family, and marriage, yet it was now difficult to walk into church by myself. I still find it difficult two years after my husband's passing.

You will need to discover who you are without your spouse. It can be an adventure or a nightmare, depending on how you approach the journey.

Just be aware of what normal grief looks like and how you are handling your own grief. Never be ashamed to ask for help or seek counseling. Many helpful grief support groups are available. In a group, you will be with others who understand what you are going through and can offer good advice and counsel. If you go to one group and feel uncomfortable, try another. Each group will have its own personality. Find the group that is right for you, where you feel most comfortable.

CHAPTER 3

Who Am I Without You?

> *"The hardest part of healing after you have lost someone you love, is to recover the "you" that went away with them."*
>
> **Author Unknown**

GROWING UP TOGETHER

W HEN YOU MARRY young, you literally grow up together. Gary spent a year on his own while going to trade school but was living at home when we got married. I went from high school graduation in May to marriage in September. We basically went from being kids living at home to being married. Our adult lives and maturity were molded as we grew up together. When I look back, I realize how mature we both were for our ages, compared to youth now. I am not sure, however, that our parents would have agreed with that assessment!

Our character and judgements were developed as we grew up together as husband and wife. Maturing that way tightly weaves you together as one. We had never made an adult decision in our lives before our decision to get married. There are a lot of joys in getting married young. You are not jaded by bad relationships, and you have no preconceived ideas about marriage. (Only what you have seen in your parents.) In our fifty years of marriage, neither of us ever had any regrets about our decision to marry young. After losing Gary, I was thankful for all the time we had together.

Some of the positives of marrying young are all the "firsts" you experience together. Your first car, your first home, your first pet, and your first savings account. There were no arguments about money since we did not have much, but our money was always a joint venture. It was never his money or her money, it was just our money. All our adult memories and experiences were shared over a lifetime. That not only makes the grief harder, but it also makes figuring out who you are seem impossible at times.

OPPOSITES ATTRACT

Gary and I got married so quickly, I am sure we did not realize how opposite our personalities were. They say opposites attract. Perhaps that is why we fell in love so easily and quickly. We were opposite in absolutely every way. I have always felt that was what made us so strong *together*. Surprisingly, our opposite personalities never seemed to cause us any problems. (Well, major problems, anyway!) We could discuss a topic, see it from two different angles, and gain a better perspective. His calm, easygoing nature kept my type A hyper personality in check.

And his laid-back easy-going nature was challenged by trying to keep up with me! We both felt, over time, we had made each other better people. We lived, loved, and learned to do life together. I have no doubts Gary made me a better person!

Who Are We?

At one point in Gary's illness, I remember thinking, *who are "we?"* The illness had changed the dynamic of who we were as a couple. We had always been busy in ministry and had no notion of ever retiring. We were just going to slow down and do something different. Our entire married life, I had always felt Gary would out-live me, because he was NEVER sick, and his Mom lived to be 92! After age fifty, I had a list of medical problems. I was diagnosed with type 2 diabetes, high blood pressure, high cholesterol, neuropathy, and thyroid problems. My family did not have good longevity. My Mom died at 68 and my Dad at 72.

So here we were, both retired due to medical issues, and Gary only given 3 to 5 years to live. Gary was in a wheelchair, with a feeding tube enabling him to eat and a trach to help him breath. How had this happened? We learned that life could change very quickly, and we needed to enjoy every moment we had left.

A New Sadness

A new sadness came over me. A sadness I could not shake. As we tried to prepare for what we knew was coming, I could not think past one day at a time. The future was too bleak and scary. How can I even go on without Gary? He had always been my strength and protector. He was my best friend — someone I could talk to about anything. He was my encourager and champion! This new sadness was not depression, but just the sadness that came from trying to wrap my mind around who we had become and where life was taking us. When Gary got his diagnosis, he said, "Vickie, we are all terminal." I knew that was true, but it was still hard to face the fact that he, at no fault of his own, was going to leave me too soon.

At some point in time, I was able to get my act together and stay positive for him. He was being so brave and positive for the rest of us, how could I do any less? My sadness turned into acceptance, which helped me make the best of each day we were given. We both knew and believed God could heal him at any moment and we constantly made that our prayer. But the time came when we had to consider this might not be the journey God wants for us. I am not saying God caused the ALS, but I am saying God does sometimes allow unwelcome things in our lives for reasons we do not understand. In the end, we know that even our times of suffering can eventually bring glory to the Father.

> *"In the darkest times of our lives,*
> *God's love and truth will shine the clearest."*
>
> **Corrie Ten Boom**

When your spouse experiences a lengthy terminal illness, you often go through some of the stages of grief while your loved one is still with you. Over the seven years of Gary's illness, I had gone through denial, anger, depression, and was now in the acceptance stage — although I did not realize or recognize the stages as I experienced them. I soon discovered it did not make his passing any easier. Your heart aches just as much. But I do believe the process of grief was different. By the time Gary died, we were all praying for God to peacefully take him home. He had suffered enough, and he was ready for it to be over. His death came as somewhat of a relief, but that did not make it any less painful. With a terminal illness, you may experience grief a little differently, but it is never any easier.

DISCOVERY YOUR STRENGTH AND WEAKNESSES

In every relationship there are strengths and weaknesses, but we seldom give it a lot of thought. At least I had not. Now, knowing I would someday be alone, the thought crossed my mind. Gary was the rock our family and marriage was built on. What would happen when he was gone? Gary was our stability and anchor. He was my plumbline to measure everything in the life of our family. We had made every decision together since our youth. How would I make decisions without him? And would I be able to make good decisions?

As I turned to God with my questions, He reminded me he was my anchor and plumbline. He reminded me He would never forsake me but would always be there when I needed Him. He let me know He was going to carry me when things got too hard, and I would never be alone. I had to have a new determination to draw ever closer to my God. He would be my counselor, my guide, my strong tower, my rock, and yes, since I belonged to him as part of the Bride of Christ, he would be my husband. I had put too much emphasis on my loss and not on what God had done and was doing for me. He was still answering my prayer and showing himself strong to Gary and me.

> *"The name of the Lord is a strong tower;*
> *the righteous run to it and are safe."*
>
> **Proverbs 18:10 (NKJ)**

CHAPTER 4

Life Re-Calibrated

❦

"Grief never ends, but it changes. It is a passage, not a place to stay. Grief is not a sign of weakness, nor a lack of faith, it is the price of love."

Author Unknown

IT STILL HURTS

AT SOME POINT in your grief, you begin to wonder if it will ever stop hurting. There are days when it will hurt physically. Grief can be overwhelming at times. You cannot imagine going on without your spouse, although you know it is your only option. You try to stay busy, but somedays *busy* does not help. Your thoughts are exploding with memories — good memories, yet they hurt. Everywhere you look, everything you do, each decision and choice, all remind you of your loved one. Your memories fill every corner of your life and mind. When you marry young and have a lifetime bond, all your adult memories are intertwined with your spouse. All your memories are the two of you as "one."

I am in my second year of my grief journey, and it still hurts, but it is getting better. I still cry often when speaking of my love, but some tears are cleansing and healing. At first, I would apologize with every tear, but not now. The first year I did not take many phone calls, because they all ended in tears. Now I can talk about Gary and enjoy the memories. The tears still flow, but they bring with them a healing for my soul.

> *"Blessed are those who mourn*
> *for they will be comforted."*
>
> *Matthew 5:4*

THINGS THAT MAY HELP....
JOURNALING MY BLESSINGS

Always remember: your life has changed, but it is not over. Here are some ideas that might help you cope with your loss.

Journaling can be helpful in keeping you in a right frame of mind. My first year, I decided to write at least five blessings each day. That was all I could manage. I found journaling kept me in a positive frame of mind and helped me be thankful for what I had. My first day of recording my blessings, I wrote this:

1.) I am thankful for the fifty years God gave me with such a wonderful husband and for my blessed marriage with Gary.

2.) I am thankful to have loved and been loved.

3.) I am thankful for the blessed hope of heaven and that I will see Gary again.

4.) I am thankful for my loving Savior, Jesus Christ.

5.) I am thankful my children and grandchildren love God.

6.) I am thankful for every day of life to draw closer to God.

Recording my blessings that first year helped my heart heal and my spirit be renewed by God's love. Remembering your blessings will help guide your future. God has a perfect plan designed just for your life, and your past blessings will give you the faith to continue following God. Never let fear block a blessing. As you are searching for who you are, be brave and courageous, and step out in faith, trusting God to guide you and always be there by your side.

RECORDING MY GOD ENCOUNTERS

After the first year, I started journaling what I called, "*My God Encounters.*" These were times in my life where I had seen God's hand on my life and his intervention for my good. I wanted to write them down so my children and grandchildren would remember how good God has been to our family. My "God Encounters" became my second book, titled *Daily Encounters with God*. This book is filled with stories of how God stepped in and changed my life. Writing this book was a way to remind my family of our blessings, to honor God by sharing all he has done for me, and to spotlight how he has shown himself strong in my life, marriage, and family.

REACHING OUT TO OTHERS

After my first year and a half of journaling, I decided to see if I could handle some volunteer work. I signed up with hospice and was introduced to my friend Gloria and her husband, Clayton. Gloria had many of the same symptoms Gary had, so it was easy to relate to her and to Clayton, her caregiver. My weekly visits with Gloria proved to be the best grief therapy I could have asked for. She would ask me questions about Gary and talking with Gloria brought much healing to my soul. Gloria encouraged me to write about our family's ALS journey when even the thought of writing a book was terrifying to me. I will be forever grateful for her and Clayton's friendship at a critical time in my life. I finished that first book, *Finding Joy in the Journey,* because of their faith in me, and because it was God ordained and inspired. All praise goes to God!

I also began preparing a monthly meal for the families at the Ronald McDonald House. I like to cook, and they needed people to prepare meals, so it was a perfect fit. I enjoyed meeting the families and listening to their stories. Many of their stories were heart breaking, but I found these people to be brave in the face of their adversities.

Doing something for someone else is our Christian mandate. It helps to keep our focus on others and not always on our own situation. Serving others will make you more thankful and help you grow spiritually. We all need the help of others, so why not be that person for someone else.

Use Your Talents and Strengths

We do not always recognize our own talents and strengths, but we all have them. You may not think you have any talents, but you do. Some of my talents and strengths are organization, hospitality, writing, cooking, driving, painting, and giving encouragement. You may be surprised that I list cooking and driving as talents and strengths. If you have a car and can drive, you can do a lot for others. You can take them to appointments, grocery shopping, and church, just to name a few places. If you can cook or order a pizza, you can help the less fortunate or those who are sick.

When we talk about talents and strengths, our minds go to singing, dancing, playing a musical instrument or drama. Those are certainly great talents, but talents can cover a broad spectrum of skills from fixing a car to painting a room! Anything you can do and use to help others is a talent.

Helping others is a great way to take our minds off ourselves. It can bring healing where you need healing. In giving, we receive. Pray about your talents and strengths and ask God what you can do for others.

These things were helpful for me to move forward in my grief. Remembering and journaling all my blessings kept me positive. Recording my "God Encounters" built up my faith. Reaching out to others helped me voice my love and grief.

You can use these ideas or come up with what helps you move forward in your grief. Our loss and grief will never be over, but we can learn to live with it and have the peace of God. Keep your eyes on Christ, the author and finisher of your faith! (Hebrew 12:2)

BE TRUE TO YOURSELF

As you journey through grief, trying to find out who you are, be honest and true to yourself. Do not try to be who others think you should be. Seek God and try new things in your process of self-discovery. I found I was not the people person I thought I was. With Gary at my side, I could be a people person, but without him, being with people became difficult and caused me anxiety.

Someone asked me, "Do you come alive around people or do they wear you out?" I had never given it much thought, but I knew instantly that they wear me out. I love people and love serving others, but I realized being around a lot of people for extended amounts of time was exhausting. When you have lost your spouse, it seems to place you in the limelight where you feel people are watching you. When I was with Gary, I gained strength from him. By myself, I did not last long before feeling drained emotionally.

I began trying new things to figure out what I might enjoy, and what I might be good at. I went to some painting classes and found I enjoyed painting and was surprisingly good. I went to a pottery class and discovered it was too hard on my hands and arms, and I was neither strong enough nor good at that. I did volunteer work and realized I did not like nursing home visits, but I did like one-on-one visits in a private setting.

One of the most peculiar and uncomfortable situations for me was going to church. My husband was a pastor, so why was it so difficult? I concluded it was because it was such a familiar place and one I equated with Gary, and that made it feel awkward and uncomfortable. I felt lost without him in that situation. It seems crazy, but it is still one of the most difficult things for me to do.

I tried my hand at writing — something I had always enjoyed but never had the time to pursue. I loved it and could spend all day writing and never get tired of it. I do not think I am the most talented or gifted writer, but I know God will equip us for anything he wants us to do. I want to continue writing, with God's help. I am amazed at all the thoughts and ideas pouring into my head! I never dreamed I would write even one book and here I am on book three! This achievement has only been possible by God's great love and his design. He has given me the desire to write something worthy— something that will bring Him glory, as well as help others. When God is in a project, he will make your way straight and your path clear.

THE NEW ME – A NEW BEGINNING

No matter where you are in life, you are just beginning. We begin again at every stage and chapter of life. Really and truly, each day is a new beginning — another chance to get it right! We should endeavor always to look forward, not behind. Your past will enhance and guide your future but should never control your future. God will use all our life experiences for his glory and honor if we allow him. After two and a half years on my journey through grief, I am a little closer to knowing who I am. I know my journey of discovery will take more time. How much more time, I do not know. I understand more about who I am now than I did two years ago. As each new situation arises, I learn more about who I am as "Me" without Gary. It is a peculiar feeling to not know and understand yourself completely at my age. Here are some of the things I have learned about myself.

1. I am uncomfortable in new situations.
2. I am not the people person I thought I was.
3. I have talents I did not know.
4. I am not as strong as others think I am.
5. I hate living alone.
6. I am more capable than I would have given myself credit.
7. I can handle a lot more than I thought I could.
8. I am a positive thinker most of the time.
9. Grief has increased my faith and relationship with Christ.

10. I can write a book and be an author!
11. I can do all things with the help of Christ, and I know he loves me!
12. I can make good decisions on my own.
13. I am brave!

This is not an exhaustive list by any means. These are some of the things I have learned about myself and am still learning. Perhaps they can help you learn about the "Me" you are without your spouse. Grief can make us stronger and wiser and can reveal to us our real strengths and courage as we are being tested.

CHAPTER 5

Where to From Here?

❧

"It takes faith to go where God wants you to go, and it takes faith to stay where God wants you to stay."

Mark Hankins

DARE TO DREAM

GOD IS NEVER finished with you until your last breath. Your age or stage of life does not matter. God will use you if you allow Him. I have discovered, as a 70-year-old widow, God still wants me to dream big. Your dreams are only as big as your God. When God asks us to do something, he will also equip us.

I am reminded of a conversation Moses had with God. God appeared in a burning bush to talk to Moses. He wanted Moses to lead his people out of Egypt, but Moses did not feel qualified. He said to God, "Who am I that I should go before Pharaoh and bring the children of Israel out of Egypt?"

God was asking Moses to lead over 600,000 men out of Egypt, in addition to their families and all their animals. It was a monumental undertaking. Knowing those numbers and the magnitude of the task, Moses continued to question God. "Who shall I say sent me?" God told Moses to tell them, "*I Am* hath sent me unto you." Then Moses said that he was slow of speech and would not know what to say. God reminded Moses that He had made his mouth, and He would give him the words to say. There was nothing left for Moses to object to. You can read the full story in Exodus 3-4.

God seldom calls the most obvious person to a monumental assignment. He calls the person who will be obedient, and who will need to depend on God if the assignment is to be completed. Then, when the assignment is completed, everyone will know it was accomplished only by the hand of God.

Consider our two widows, Naomi, and Ruth. God used Ruth, the Moabite woman, to be in the lineage of David and Jesus. The Israelites looked down on the Moabites and considered them to be the least of the least. Yet God chose Ruth.

And whom did God choose to defeat Goliath? There was an entire army of grown men available, but God chose a shepherd boy because of his heart of obedience. Some of God's unlikely choices were Noah, a drunkard, to build the ark to save humanity; Abraham, at age 100, to be the Father of many nation; Moses, who stuttered, to be His spokesman to Pharaoh, and Rahab, a prostitute, to be included in the lineage of the Messiah. We cannot forget

David on our list of unlikely people. David was an adulterer and a murderer, yet God chose him to be an ancestor of our Messiah. Jonah was disobedient and ran away from God's assignment, but God never gave up on him or Nineveh. We can also include Matthew, the tax collector, and Saul, who persecuted Christians.

Perhaps God's most unlikely choice, to the human mind, was Jesus himself. He came as a baby, not as a conquering warrior. He grew up in a carpenter's home, not in a palace. He had nothing to offer his followers but a cross. In the eyes of the Jewish leaders, he was a religious imposter. He died like a criminal. Yet through his obedience, many were made righteous, and the door of heaven was opened to "whosoever."

When God calls you to do something you think beyond your capability, remember our list of unlikely people in the Bible and stand tall in your obedience. Remember, whatever God asks you to do, he will equip you and supply all you need to get the job done.

DREAM BIG!

When I realized God was speaking to me about writing and sharing our family's story about our ALS journey, I reacted much like Moses. I felt it was out of my scope of ability and far beyond my talents. God and I had many conversations, but in the end, I was willing. I knew if I were able to write a book, it would be accomplished only by God's grace and design. I followed the dream God gave me and wrote my first book, *Finding Joy in The Journey*. My prayer upon completion of that first book was, "God, please bless every hand that touches this book and be glorified in their lives." Should this book become a success, it will be God alone who caused that success! My only boast is in Christ.

> "It is not my ability, but my response to God's ability, that counts!"
>
> **Author Unknown**

GOD IS NOT THROUGH WITH YOU YET!

God is not through with you yet. No matter how old you are, the best is yet to come! We often hear older people in the church say, "I have done my part. It is time for the younger people to step up." The truth is, we are all supposed to be about our Father's business. Every generation can and should contribute. That is what makes up a heathy church. Older women are called to teach the younger women, and older men are to teach the younger men. I watched my husband, while bedridden, continue to serve his God. He prayed for people, wrote, and encouraged others. He even had a praise service and communion right in our bedroom. If he could do that from his bed, while unable to walk, talk, or breathe on his own, we all should be able to contribute to the Kingdom of God. It goes back to knowing your talents and finding out where God wants to use you.

When you find yourself trying to justify why you cannot do something God has asked of you, remember these people. Corrie Ten Boom, in her eighties, was still sharing how God saved her life while in the German prison camp.

Joni Eareckson Tada, who writes books, sings, paints, and speaks from her wheelchair, is quadriplegic. Helen Keller lived a productive life, although she was born blind and deaf. And how about James Vujicic? He is a motivational speaker who was born without arms or legs. We cannot forget Walt Disney, who had one failure after another, yet kept dreaming This is by no means an exhaustive list of people who have overcome great odds and been successful. They, and many more like them, dared to dream and use what they had to make things happen. They discovered, with God, what they had was enough.

Never give up your dreams. If anything, dream bigger! Our God is able!

Your New Assignment

We all have a desire to find meaning in our lives. When you lose someone you love, at first it feels like life is over, but let me assure you, it is not. As we are discovering who we are (the new "Me"), we will also realize God still has a plan and purpose for us to fulfill. In that discovery, your life will begin to bloom once again. As we give ourselves to God, he will show us his will and purpose. He has a plan for every day of our lives, and he will reveal it if we simply seek him and ask. Our purpose is to share the Gospel with a lost and dying world. God will use you in ways he can use no one else. His plan for your life lies in your uniqueness, your talents, and your life experiences. God sees all you are and has designed a plan and purpose for you that only you can accomplish. Following God's design is exciting and new each day. (Jeremiah 29:11)

As you adapt to widowhood, God will have a new assignment waiting for you when you feel you are ready. Take your time, pray about it, and do not rush into anything until you are sure. It has always been hard for me to not get out ahead of God, but as a widow, I am taking my time to get it right. I want to be doing what God wants, not what I think I should be doing. When I follow God's lead, I will be making eternal investments. I am also not rushing, because I want to be sure I am at a place where I can handle things emotionally. God will never rush you. You want to be ready — physically, emotionally, and spiritually. Only you and God will know when the time is right. You can be sure God will awaken a dream in your heart and stir you to action when it is his time. Remember, no matter your age, God has a perfect plan just for your life. He will use your experiences to bless others. John 8:12 tells us we are to be the light of the world, showing others the way to the saving knowledge of Jesus Christ. We must get out there and let our light shine as only ours can.

> *"I am the light of the world. Whoever follows me will-never walk in darkness but will have the light of life."*
>
> *John 8:12*

David Jeremiah's book, *Forward*, is about not living in the past, but pressing on in what God has for us to do. One of my favorite lines in the book is: "When you serve the Kingdom of Heaven, your future is unfolding at the speed of Grace." Serving God is exciting and new each day. As we wait on the Lord in anticipation of our next assignment, it is amazing to see what unfolds. At my age, and as a widow, it is such a joy to be used by God. When I see my Jesus face to face, I want to know I have run a good race. I want to hear his "Well done," and I want to find many rewards awaiting me. The awards are not for the sake of my accomplishments, which are worthless without Christ. He is my only boast and champion in this life. I want to be able to lay my rewards at his feet as my "Thank you" for all he has done in my life. No matter how many awards await me, they will never be enough in comparison to all He has done for me. As the song says:

> "Oh, how he loves you and me,
> Oh, how he loves you and me.
> He gave his life, what more could he give?
> Oh, how he loves you, oh how he loves me.
> Oh, how he loves you and me."

CHAPTER 6

For Such a Time as This

⚜

Mordecai said to Esther, "And who knows whether you
have attained royalty for such a time as this?"
Esther 4:14

BE EXPECTANT, BE EXCITED, BE OBEDIENT, BE READY AND BE WILLING!

MOVING ON AFTER a loss is not easy. Some days, just getting out of bed seems impossible. Eventually, you will come to the place in your grief where you are ready once again for God to use you, and you will desire a purpose in your life. Moving on after your loss requires courage, strength, and faith. To go forward into the unknown, we must have a confidence that can only come from our faith in God.

Be expectant in your new purpose and direction. Take advantage of every opportunity God gives, no matter how big the challenge. It will take all the courage you have for each step. As you launch out into the world as a widow, it will be different than anything you have experienced before. You will feel like you are alone, but you are not. God is right there beside you, cheering for you!

Be Excited in finding your new purpose. God will guide you as you read and study his Word for your directions. As you are seeking God, don't underestimate your gifts, talents, and life experiences. God will use them for his purpose and glory. If you are a people person, he might ask you to reach out in ways only you can. He might use you to teach a bible study, lead a small prayer group, or do hospital visitation. Always keep in mind, when God gives you an assignment, your faith is going to be tested and stretched. In the process, we grow and are changed from glory to glory. God is famous for giving assignments to the least likely person. Wherever God leads you, your willingness and obedience will count more than your abilities in bringing glory to the Father.

Be Obedient to God's call and design for your life. When God calls you, he will equip you. You can be sure you will be blessed. If you are not obedient in what he asks, he will ask someone else. Remember, blessing is found in your obedience. Do not miss your blessing! You may experience some failures along the way, but just keep moving forward and do not look back. God is more concerned with your obedience than he is worried about your failures. Paul said he was forgetting the past to move on toward the high calling of Christ.

"Forgetting what is behind and straining toward what
is ahead, I press on toward the goal to win the prize for
which God has called me heavenward in Christ Jesus."
Philippians 3:14

Paul knew that dwelling on past mistakes only serves to distract you from what God wants you to do today. The older I get, and the more experienced in life, I realize how much more I can trust God to know what is best for me and for those around me.

Be Ready for what God has in store for your future. God often asks us to step out of our comfort zone and do something that will require total trust in him. His choice for us is seldom what we would have chosen. It may be something you do not feel qualified to accomplish. (Like me writing a book!) Be ready and willing to rely on God in everything. As we fall in love with him more each day, we will learn to trust him in anything he asks of us. When I get to Heaven, I want to hear Christ say,

"Well done, good and faithful servant: you have been
faithful over a few things, I will make you ruler over
many things, enter into the joy of the Lord."
Matthew 25:21

I want to work hard now, while I can, and achieve as many heavenly rewards as possible. I am not a competitive person , but I want those rewards so I can lay them at the feet of my Jesus, to thank him for all he has done for me! Then I will get in line for my next assignment in heaven as an even newer and revised version of "Me"! God's word tells us, because we were faithful in a few things, he will make us rulers over many things. The assignments may have a different purpose than here on earth, but I am convinced they will give us the sense of accomplishment and joy we were created for and desire — forever giving glory to our God.

Be willing servants now, while you can still deposit treasures in Heaven. The Bible tells us about the rewards that await us. They are referred to as crowns. The "Victor's Crown," mentioned in 1 Corinthians 9:4-25, is given to those who have led a disciplined and godly life. The "Crown of Rejoicing," mentioned in 1 Thessalonians 2:2-19, is given to those who have influenced others on earth by their deeds, words, and love. There will be great joy in seeing those people in heaven! A "Crown of Righteousness," spoken of in 2 Timothy 4:8, is given to those who have developed an intense desire for the Lord's return and have longed for his appearing. James tells us about the "Crown of Life" in James 1:12. This crown is given to all who endured and overcame temptations and trials. And finally, the "Crown of Glory," mentioned in 1 Peter 5:4, is given to all who were willing and eager to serve and care for the body of Christ. We have many opportunities for rewards while we still have time to work here on earth. What a joy it will be to see in heaven the people our lives have touched and influenced while here on earth.

These are the crowns we will be able to lay at the feet of Jesus in praise and thanksgiving for all he has done. What a sight that will be! I pray I will be able to lay my crowns there, at Jesus' feet, and contribute to the celebration of praise, adoration, and thanksgiving to our Savior and Lord.

God asks us to be expectant, excited, obedient, and ready! He will use the adversities of this life as an opportunity to advance his redemptive purposes. We never suffer in vain, because God will turn our sorrow and tears into joy for His Kingdom and His eternal purpose. Our greatest rewards and best days are still ahead.

> *"God is not through with you yet! Count the cost and step out into the unknown trusting God. Watch and see what the Lord will do. He is going to take you to a place you never thought possible and use you in ways you never could have dreamed. The best is yet to come. So, dream big."*
>
> *"Me"*

GRIEF IS...
by Roberta Bonnici

Grief is the agonizing question, "My God, why...?"
  It is the empty place in the bed beside you –
    silent crib.
    The vacant rocker.
    The extra space at the table.
Grief is the product of a lost love,
    A lost friendship,
    A lost dream,
    Or a lost opportunity.
Grief is the realization that part of you is gone.
  It is the frantic knocking on the door of the past,
  only to be answered by the wraith of memory.

Grief calls forth the moisture in your eyes,
    The dryness in your throat,
    The weight on your chest.
Grief renders food tasteless,
    dismisses sleep,
    and wraps the total self in its own anesthesia.
Grief is a sob,
  A sigh,
    A moan.
      A groping for meaning.
        The mixed desire to be – and not to be.

Grief is the endless yearning for a familiar face, voice, and touch.

Grief is the haunting dream that seems so real yet mocks reality.
Grief is the analysis of "What if…?" and "If only…"
Grief is the anger that demands to know, "Is this the work of a loving God?"
Grief is the slow plodding through another day – a mechanical existence.
Grief is staring into the black abyss of the soul, waiting for the raw, throbbing ache to go away.

Grief is all of this. And yet,
    It is also the acquiescence to life.
    Reaching out to those who offer help.
    Clinging to the symbols of hope.
    Remembering the suffering of Christ.

Grief is the acceptance of what has happened and
    the willingness to go on alone.
Grief is the building of memorials
    In the cemetery,
        In society,
            In the secret chambers of the self.
Grief is the gradual understanding that some things never die –
    That love is, indeed, eternal.

Grief is turning to the light and discovering the tears have formed a rainbow.
Grief is drawing from the fragments of yesterday to build today.

It is finding new strength and meaning in that which remains.
It is the realignment of goals, priorities, motives, and desires.

Grief can be a Taj Mahal – or a Potter's Field.
It is the testing of all that has made us what we are.
Grief is the raw emotion from which we construct either heaven or hell.
Grief is the chastening of the soul –
The cleansing that leads to tomorrow.

 CPSIA information can be obtained
at www.ICGtesting.com
Printed in the USA
BVHW080756160621
609629BV00003B/376